FOCUS ON

AIR

BARBARA TAYLOR

Aladdin/Watts
London • Sydney

This edition published in 2003
© Aladdin Books Ltd 2003

Designed and produced by
Aladdin Books Ltd
28 Percy Street
London W1T 2BZ

First published in
Great Britain in 1994 by
Watts Books
96 Leonard Street
London EC2A 4XD

ISBN 0 7496 5073 7

A CIP catalogue record for this book is
available from the British Library.

Printed in UAE

Design	David West Children's Book Design
Designer	Flick Killerby
Series director	Bibby Whittaker
Editor	Jim Pipe
Picture research	Brooks Krikler Research
Illustrator	Dave Burroughs

The author, Barbara Taylor, has a degree in
science, and has written and edited many
books for children, mainly on science
subjects.

The consultant, Dr Bryson Gore, is a
lecturer and lecturers' superintendent at
The Royal Institution, London.

INTRODUCTION

The mixture of gases we call the air is
essential to life on Earth, forming an
atmospheric protective blanket which
extends 900km from the surface of the
Earth. People have changed the
composition of the atmosphere with
pollution, yet air continues to provide all
living things with the means to create and
use the energy they need to live and grow.
Air also keeps the Earth warm enough for
life to survive. Moving air, called the
wind, is a vital ingredient in our ever-
changing weather. This book explores the
scientific properties of air and aims to
provide a comprehensive picture of the
composition of air, how we use it and its
importance to living things. The key
below explains the format of the book.

Geography
The symbol of the planet
Earth shows where
geographical facts and activities
are included. These panels
include a look at how air
changes with altitude and how
this affects animal breathing
and plant life.

Language and literature
An open book is the sign for
activities which involve language
and literature. One such panel
explores common air sayings
while another looks at Ancient
Greek beliefs. A further box
looks at William Shakespeare's
The Tempest, inspired by wind.

Science
The microscope symbol indicates where a science project or science information is given. For example, one panel looks at different forms of green power, such as sails and wind farms.

History
The sign of the scroll and hourglass shows where historical information is given. These sections aim to provide an insight into man's relationship with the air through the ages, such as the histories of windmills and kites.

Maths
A ruler and compass indicate maths information and activities. Included in these panels is a look at noise pollution in the air and how it is measured. Also discussed is how the speed of sound through the air is used as a unit of speed.

Arts, crafts and music
The symbol showing a sheet of music and art tools signals arts, crafts or musical activities. Topics covered include musical tunes with air as their theme, and how an artist's airbrush works. Also included is a project to build a model glider.

CONTENTS

WHAT IS AIR?

Air is everywhere on Earth, even inside our own bodies. We cannot see, smell or hear air but our lives would be very different without it. Air causes changes in the weather, keeps things warm or cool, lets fires burn and allows sounds to travel. Air consists of a mixture of gases, mainly nitrogen and oxygen, and can be squashed or compressed into small spaces. The air is constantly recycled by nature – so the air we breathe today is the same air that helped plants to grow millions of years ago (above left).

Gases in the air

Most of the air, about 78 per cent, is nitrogen gas. About 21 per cent is oxygen gas. All living things need oxygen to release energy from their food. The remaining 1 per cent of the air consists of gases such as carbon dioxide, argon, neon, helium, krypton, hydrogen, xenon and ozone. The carbon dioxide in the air helps to keep the Earth warm. The air also contains dust, and moisture in the form of water vapour.

Argon and other gases 1%

Nitrogen 78%

Oxygen 21%

Humidity

The amount of water vapour in the air is called its humidity. As air cools down, some of the water vapour turns into liquid water, called condensation. This happens because cool air holds less water vapour than warm air. Condensation may cause clouds, fog or dew to form.

Early morning dew

Pressure

Barometers (see above) measure air pressure, which is caused by the force of gravity pulling the air down towards the Earth's surface. Changes in air pressure signal changes in the weather. High pressure usually indicates fine, settled weather, while low pressure usually means cloudy, rainy weather.

Air studies

Before the 1700s, air was thought to be a pure substance. However, in 1754, Joseph Black discovered carbon dioxide in air. Oxygen was found by Carl Scheele in the early 1770s and by Joseph Priestly (shown right) in 1774. Nitrogen was discovered in 1772 by Daniel Rutherford, but inert gases such as argon were not detected until the 1890s.

Air particles
In a shaft of sunlight, you can often see dust floating in the air. Air always contains many tiny solid particles, from car exhausts, factory smoke, and forest fires. Other sources include pollen from plants and salt from the sea. Polluted air over a large city may contain billions of particles.

Feeding a fire
Fires need the oxygen in the air to burn. People sometimes blow on a fire to give it more oxygen. To put out a fire, they cut off the supply of oxygen by spraying it with water, foam or carbon dioxide.

Rusty pipes
If iron or steel are exposed to air and moisture, they usually rust and the metal is eaten away. Rust happens when iron joins up with oxygen in the air to form iron oxide. Protective paint can stop oxygen from reaching iron or steel and therefore stops rusting taking place.

Air sayings

The word air is often used in sayings to convey different meanings. For instance, 'to walk on air' is to feel elated and for something 'to be in the air' means it is uncertain.

Can you find out the meanings of these sayings: to go on the air; to take the air; to give yourself airs; an airy-fairy idea; to be an airhead?

See if you can compose a poem or a song using some common air sayings.

Useful gases

The gases in the air can be collected separately by a process called fractional distillation. Air is made into a liquid by being cooled to very low temperatures. When it warms up, the gases boil off the liquid at different times because they have different boiling points.

Liquid oxygen is used for powering rockets. Oxygen gas (left) is used in breathing apparatus for fire-fighters and the sick.

Nitrogen gas is used to make fertilisers (above right), while nitric acid (a compound of nitrogen and sulphate dissolved in water) is a key ingredient in explosives.

Argon is used to fill the space in most light bulbs as it is an extremely unreactive (or inert) gas.

Green plants use carbon dioxide to make their own food. Carbon dioxide fire extinguishers are used to put out fires in burning liquids and electrical fires. Carbon dioxide also provides the 'fizz' in many fizzy drinks.

Neon, another colourless, odourless inert gas, is used in fluorescent signs and strip lighting.

Helium is a very light, inert gas used to fill modern airships. It is also used for some types of party balloon.

AIR AND THE EARTH

The Earth is surrounded by the atmosphere, a big layer of air which formed about 4,500 million years ago. It is held in place by the pull of the Earth's gravity. The atmosphere works like a shield, keeping out harmful rays from the Sun and reducing the impact of rocks from space as they fly towards the Earth's surface. Life is only possible on Earth because the atmosphere prevents it getting too hot or cold.

Measuring air pressure

Atmospheric pressure is endlessly changing – it pushes on us from all directions because of the gas molecules constantly jostling with each other.

To feel the effect of atmospheric pressure try this simple test. Place a piece of paper flat on a table, by the edge. Then slip a ruler between the paper and the table and lever the paper upwards with the ruler. The force you feel working against you is atmospheric pressure.

Colours of the sky

Sunlight is composed of all the colours of the rainbow. Molecules of gas in the atmosphere scatter the blue light more than the other colours. So extra blue light reaches our eyes and we see the sky as blue on clear days.

At sunrise or sunset, the Sun is low in the sky and has to shine through a thicker layer of atmosphere. More light is scattered aside by dust and gas molecules in the air and only the orange and red light gets through.

On the Moon, the sky looks black because there is no atmosphere with dust and gases to scatter the light.

Layers in the atmosphere

The atmosphere can be divided into five main layers, although there are no physical barriers and the gases in the air move freely about. More than 75 per cent of the atmosphere is in the troposphere, and all life and weather is in this layer. Above this, the stratosphere contains the ozone layer, which absorbs ultraviolet rays from the Sun. In the upper atmosphere, where the air is very thin, are the mesosphere, thermosphere and exosphere. In the thermosphere the air can reach temperatures as high as 2,000 degrees C.

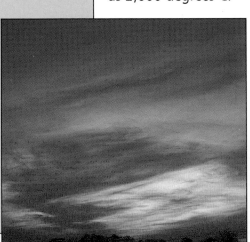

Space suits

Out in space, there is no air at all, so to travel to and from space or work outside their spacecraft, astronauts wear special space suits. These act as a kind of miniature atmosphere, providing air pressure (blood pressure would cause astronauts' bodies to explode otherwise), temperature control and pure oxygen. The early space suits used for walking on the Moon have been developed into sophisticated Manned Manoeuvring Units. First used in 1984, these have an autopilot that keeps the astronaut in position using nitrogen gas-jets.

Exosphere – up to 900km

Only 47 per cent of the total radiation from the Sun ever reaches the Earth's surface. The rest is absorbed by the ozone layer (in the stratosphere) or is reflected back into the stratosphere by clouds.

Thermosphere – up to 450km

Mesosphere – up to 80km

Stratosphere – up to 50km

Tropopause

Troposphere – up to 20km

Altitude

As you go higher and higher above the Earth, there is less and less air and the atmosphere becomes thinner. On high mountains, there is not enough oxygen in the air for climbers to breathe properly so they may take oxygen tanks with them. Mountain animals, and people living at high altitudes, develop large hearts and lungs to enable them to take more oxygen from the air.

Altitude sickness happens when people do not get enough oxygen. They may experience symptoms such as headaches, nausea, coughing and sleeplessness.

10,000m – aircraft cabins are pressurised to the equivalent of 2,000m

9,000m – maximum height people can survive without extra oxygen

4,000m – altitude sickness can occur

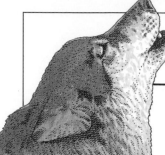

AIR AND SOUNDS

Sounds are made when something moves to and fro very quickly. This is called vibration. When something vibrates, it makes the air around it vibrate too, causing small changes in air pressure. The sounds you hear are pressure changes which reach your ears and make bones and liquids inside your ears vibrate. Out in space, there is no sound, because there is no air to carry the vibrations along, so sounds have to be converted into radio waves to travel through space. Sounds are very useful in communication and can be used to make music.

A low-pitched sound getting gradually louder

High and low sounds

High or low sounds depend on the number of sound waves per second, called the frequency. Frequency is measured in hertz (hz) – one hertz equals one vibration per second. With high notes, there are more waves per second, a higher frequency, than with low notes. High notes happen when something vibrates very fast and low notes when something vibrates slowly. Pitch is the name for how low or high a sound is.

By making their lips vibrate as they blow, trumpet players make the air in the trumpet vibrate to produce sounds. Different notes are made with tighter or looser lips and by opening and closing valves that change the length of the tube. Long columns of air make lower notes than short ones.

Concert halls

Concert halls are built to avoid unwanted echoes and sounds bumping into each other. This means sounds carry well from the stage to the audience. The shape of the hall and the materials used are important – soft, bumpy surfaces absorb sounds, while hard, flat surfaces reflect them, causing echoes. The picture on the right shows sound absorbing structures hanging from the roof of the Royal Albert Hall, London.

Human sounds

People make sounds when air passes over their vocal cords, which are flaps of skin and muscle in the throat. High sounds are made when the cords are stretched tight, low notes when they are looser. The loudness of the sounds we make depends on the amount of air passing over the vocal cords. To shape vocal sounds into words, we use the mouth, tongue and lips.

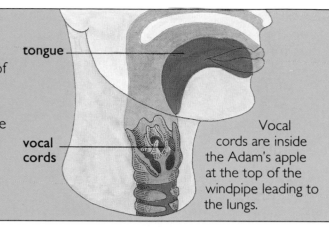

tongue

vocal cords

Vocal cords are inside the Adam's apple at the top of the windpipe leading to the lungs.

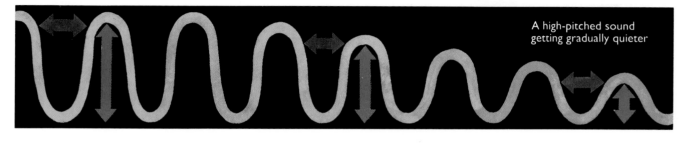

A high-pitched sound getting gradually quieter

Loud and quiet sounds

The loudness of a sound depends on the amount of energy the sound waves carry. When they are recorded on a machine called an oscilloscope, loud sounds make taller waves than quiet sounds. The height of a wave is called its amplitude.

The further away you are from a sound, the quieter it gets. This is because sound waves spread out in all directions, like the ripples from a stone thrown in a pond. They get weaker further from the source of a sound.

Supersonic planes

In 1947, Captain 'Chuck' Yaeger (below) became the first person to fly faster than the speed of sound. The speed of supersonic planes is measured in Mach numbers after physicist Ernst Mach (1838-1916). Mach 1 is equal to the speed of sound (332m per second), Mach 2 is twice the speed of sound and so on.

Storing and sending sound

The first machine for recording and playing back sound was the phonograph. It was invented by Thomas Edison in 1877. Sounds were recorded onto a drum covered in tin foil, and could be played for only about a minute. A wax cylinder was eventually developed instead and, in 1887, a flat disc. Though magnetic tape and compact cassettes offered an alternative to scratchable records in the 1970s, the compact disc of the 1980s offered the first real improvement in reproduction quality. Compact discs have patterns of microscopic pits and bumps, which are detected by a laser beam. When sent via satellite, sound waves are converted into electric waves and then into radio waves.

AIR AND ANIMALS

Without air, animals could not live for more than a few minutes. They need the oxygen from the air in their bloodstream to break down their food and release energy so they can live and grow. Food is combined with oxygen, then carbon dioxide and water are released as waste products. The process of releasing energy in this way is called respiration and it happens inside the cells (such as the red blood cells above left) that make up an animal's body. Animals have various special structures to take oxygen from air and water – we have lungs and fishes have gills.

Greek beliefs
Ancient Greek scientists believed that air was one of the four basic elements (air, water, fire and earth) from which all things were made, and that the universe was controlled by the relationship of the four elements.

With humans, air enters the body through the nose and mouth. Here the air is warmed and cleaned before it passes down the throat to the lungs. The nostrils on a whale (below left) are called blowholes after the spout of water vapour produced when they exhale. Their wide nasal passages allow quick breathing at the surface.

The lungs fill most of the chest cavity. The diaphragm (a sheet of muscle below the lungs) moves down to draw air into the lungs and up to squeeze it out. Inside the lungs are two branching tubes (the bronchi) leading to millions of air sacs, called alveoli. The alveoli in the lungs have very thin walls and are surrounded by a network of tiny tubes of blood, called capillaries. The oxygen breathed in passes easily from the alveoli into the blood. Carbon dioxide passes back in the other direction and is breathed out.

wind pipe

alveoli

bronchus

diaphragm

Breathing problems

People may have difficulty breathing if their lungs or breathing tubes are infected by bacteria or viruses. Smoking and air pollution also contribute to breathing problems, such as bronchitis and asthma. In an asthma attack, the muscles wrapped around the airways contract, restricting the flow of air and making it difficult to breathe.

Patients with breathing problems or people who are very ill are sometimes given extra oxygen. Their lungs do not have to work as hard and this helps a quicker recovery.

Insects

Air enters an insect's body through holes called spiracles, which lead to a network of tubes called tracheae and in turn to even thinner tubes that branch out to all parts of the body.

air sac

tracheae

Oxygen passes from the moist ends of the tracheoles into the insect's cells.

water is forced over the gills to produce oxygen

Fish

Most fish have gills to take in oxygen from the water around them. Some fish pump water over their gills, others swim with their mouths open so that the water is forced over the gills. Fish gills are a series of tiny flaps with a large surface area and a lot of blood vessels to help the fish absorb as much oxygen as possible into the bloodstream.

The aqualung

Invented by Jacques Cousteau and Emile Gagnan in 1943, the aqualung revolutionised underwater exploration. Divers were able to move easily, without cumbersome diving suits, and could dive to depths of up to 60m. Through an aqualung, divers breathe air at the same pressure as the surrounding water. The aqualung is also known as scuba – Self Contained Underwater Breathing Apparatus.

Aqualungs consist of cylinders of air at high pressure, a valve to control air pressure and a tube to the mouthpiece.

PLANTS AND AIR

Air is just as vital to the survival of plants as it is to animals. Plants need carbon dioxide from the air to make food during the process of photosynthesis. But they also take in oxygen from the air and give out carbon dioxide, just as animals do. The waste product of photosynthesis is oxygen, which plants release into the air. During the history of the Earth, plants gradually built up the oxygen in the atmosphere. Only after there was enough oxygen in the air, could animals develop.

oxygen

Dispersal record
You could make your own nature diary to keep a record of seeds which are spread by the wind, such as sycamore or dandelion seeds. Stick the seeds into your scrapbook and write down the date and where you found them. In spring and summer, look out for plants that use the wind to spread their pollen, such as tree catkins.

poppy seeds

Using the wind
Pollen and seeds that float on the wind are usually very light, but some use other floating devices such as little 'wings', parachutes or air sacs. Seeds move away from the parent plant to reduce the competition for light, water and food nutrients.

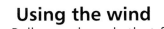

water and minerals

dandelion spores

A giant puffball can produce 7,000 billion spores in a lifetime. The spores (simple seeds) puff out in clouds every time the wind blows against them. Even an ordinary field mushroom can release 100 million spores in an hour.

Land plant roots obtain the oxygen they need from water in the soil

water

carbon dioxide

The epidermis is covered in a waxy layer called the cuticle. Though this prevents the leaf losing water, it also prevents carbon dioxide entering. So there are stomata (usually on the shady side) to let carbon dioxide in.

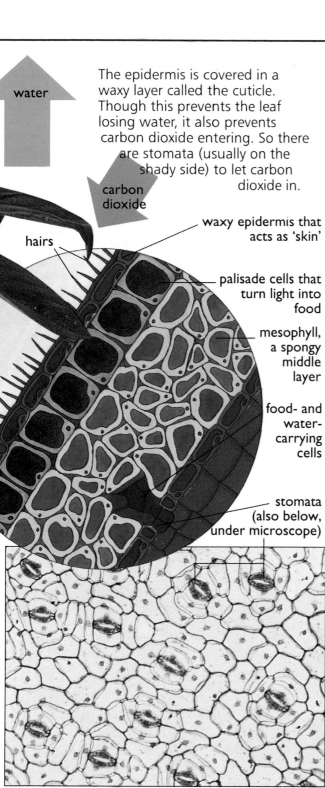

hairs

waxy epidermis that acts as 'skin'

palisade cells that turn light into food

mesophyll, a spongy middle layer

food- and water-carrying cells

stomata (also below, under microscope)

Hay fever

Many people suffer from an allergic reaction to plant pollen called hay fever. Symptoms include a runny nose, sneezing and watery eyes, but they are seasonal since plants only release pollen in spring and summer. Pollen counts are often given as part of weather forecasts to warn sufferers when to expect problems.

Plant 'breathing'

Water plants take in gases from the water all over their surface. Land plants breathe through little holes called stomata in the leaves or stem. Woody stems have small raised pores called lenticels instead of stomata. The stomata or lenticels open and close to control the flow of gases and water vapour in and out of the leaf or stem. On a leaf, the stomata are mostly on the underside. There may be from 20 to over 1,000 stomata per square millimetre, depending on the species. The stomata usually open during daylight hours when the plant is busy taking in and giving out gases during photosynthesis.

Food from air

Plants make their own food from carbon dioxide and water, using the energy in sunlight. This process is called photosynthesis. The food that plants make is a sort of sugar called a carbohydrate. Some food is broken down during respiration to release energy.

Plants on mountains

At high altitudes, there is less oxygen for plants to breathe and less carbon dioxide for them to make their food. So mountain plants tend to grow slowly and function at a slow rate. The thin mountain air also fails to protect the mountain slopes from strong sunlight during the day and cold at night. Mountain plants tend to be short to hug the ground for warmth and to trap moisture, often growing in closely packed cushions for mutual protection.

WIND AND WEATHER

From carving rocks and building sand dunes to blowing over trees and buildings, the wind has the power to change the landscape. Wind is air on the move, going from areas of high pressure to areas of low pressure. The pressure differences are created by the Sun heating up some parts of the Earth more than others. Warm air is 'lighter' or less dense than cold air, so it rises up and spreads out, creating low pressure. Dense, cold air sinks down, pressing heavily on the Earth to create high pressure.

Lows

Areas of low air pressure are called 'lows' or depressions. They happen when warm air rises, causing the pressure to drop at the Earth's surface. The rising warm air cools as it reaches higher altitudes. Cool air holds less moisture than warm air, so some of the moisture in the air condenses into droplets of water which gather to form rain clouds.

low air pressure

cool air falls to valley

warm air rises up slopes causing daytime breeze

warm rises from valley

cool air falls down slopes causing nightime breeze

day sea breeze

night sea breeze

Land and sea breezes

In mountainous regions, air on the valley floor heats up quickly during the day and rises up the slopes. At night, the air above the slopes cools more rapidly and is pulled down into the valley by gravity.

A similar reversal takes place in coastal regions. During the day hot air rises off the land and cooler air over the sea is drawn in to take its place, creating a sea breeze. At night, the sea stays warmer for longer than the land, so warm air rises over the sea and cooler air from the land is sucked in, creating a land breeze.

World winds

Winds are movements of air from areas of high pressure to low pressure. The equator is warmer than the poles, so the air rises and moves towards the poles, creating low pressure. At the cold poles, the air sinks and moves towards the equator, causing high pressure. Around the Earth, movements of air between areas of high and low pressure result in convection cells (see right). World winds do not move from the equator to the poles in straight lines because the planet is spinning in space, dragging the air with it. Winds bend to the east both north and south of the equator.

The Tempest
In *The Tempest*, written by William Shakespeare, the action takes place on a remote island, where Prospero, once Duke of Milan, uses his magic to conjure up a violent storm. During the tempest, Prospero's brother Antonio is shipwrecked on the island. With the help of the spirit Ariel, Prospero confronts Antonio (who took his dukedom) and regains his rightful position in Milan.

Forecasting the weather
Weather forecasts are vitally important for people like farmers. Short-range forecasts predict the weather for the next 24 hours and long-range forecasts predict the weather up to 8 days ahead. Information for forecasts is collected from land stations, aircraft, ships, balloons and satellites. Computer models help to predict the most likely weather.

Highs
Areas of high air pressure are called 'highs' or anticyclones. They occur where cool air sinks down to the ground and presses on the Earth's surface. The air on the surface moves away towards surrounding low pressure areas, spreading out in the form of circling winds. Whereas lows are usually associated with unsettled wet and windy weather, 'highs' usually bring fine, settled weather with light winds. This is because the air becomes warmer and drier as it sinks down.

The winds around a high in the northern hemisphere swirl clockwise. South of the equator, they circle around in the opposite direction. An elongated extension of a high is called a ridge of high pressure. An extension of a low is called a trough.

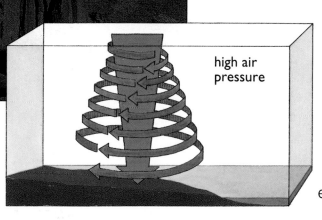

high air pressure

(Above) A desert landscape shaped by the wind

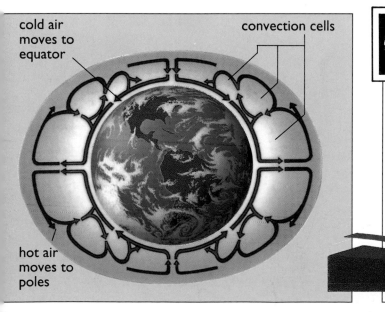

cold air moves to equator

convection cells

hot air moves to poles

Local winds
Small-scale localised winds are often given special names. For instance, the mistral is a cold north wind which funnels down the Rhône valley in France. The sirocco is a very hot, dry wind that blows off the Sahara Desert in North Africa, while the chinook blows down from the Rockies of North America.

chinook

mistral

USING THE WIND

The wind is a free, non-polluting source of energy and power which is renewable and cannot be used up, as can other energy sources such as coal or oil. People have harnessed the power of the wind for centuries. Before ships had engines, all large ships were pushed along when the wind filled their sails. Windmills also catch the wind in their sails, using the movement to grind corn, pump water or generate electricity. Many leisure activities, such as sailing, windsurfing and kite flying, rely on wind power.

Green power
Modern windmills can generate enough electricity to supply whole towns or villages, but large numbers have to be grouped together. However, these huge 'wind farms' look ugly and spoil the landscape. In addition, they can only work where there are strong winds and then only when the wind blows. A form of green power that has been used for much longer is the sails on boats and ships. The direction in which a sailing boat moves depends on the sideways 'lift' produced by the sail, the way the water pushes against the hull and the position of the rudder. The sail acts in a similar way to a wing, with the 'lift' being produced by low air pressure on one side of the sail.

Windmills
The first record of a farmer using a windmill to grind corn comes from Persia (modern-day Iran) in AD 644. Early windmills were called post mills because they rested on a big upright post. The miller had to push the mill around to keep the sails facing into the wind. Later mills, built after the mid-1700s, had the sails in a cap on top of the mill. In the rear of the cap was a small set of sails called a fantail which turned the cap around to face the wind (see picture right). These were called either smock or tower mills.

fantail

Winds of change

How many sayings can you think of which use the word wind? The 'winds of change' means a tendency for reform, while to 'take the wind out of somebody's sails' is to frustrate them by anticipating their arguments.

Other common sayings include: It's an ill wind that blows no good; to have the wind up; to scatter to the four winds; like the wind; to be a windbag!

Tiny spiders, or spiderlings, are so light they float on the air. They spin threads of silk and drift on the wind away from their mother to look for a new home of their own.

Kites

Kites are the oldest flying machines. The Chinese flew kites 2,500 years ago to frighten their enemies or to test the wind. They built kites large enough to carry people aloft. In Europe, children have flown kites for over 1,000 years. There are different shapes of kites, from the traditional diamond shapes, to stable box kites or delta wing kites, now used for stunt kite flying.

In Japan, traditional kites are decorated with animal symbols or characters from legends. Japanese o-dako fighting kites are controlled by up to 50 lines worked by twelve people. Nagasaki fighting kites have only one line, but this is coated with glue mixed with powdered glass. Contestants try to cut through each other's lines by manoeuvring their kite below their rival's kite.

Modern windmills for generating electricity are called wind turbines. They look like giant propellers on the top of a tall tower. Generating electricity like this does not pollute the atmosphere, but the turbines do tend to be very noisy.

FLOATING ON AIR

Hot-air balloons, gliders and parachutes all help us to
float on air without using any real power. They make use
of rising currents of hot air or take advantage of air
resistance or drag to slow down the rate at which
they fall down through the air. Air resistance is caused by the force of
air pushing against something and slowing it down. Some gliding
animals are also capable of unpowered flight.

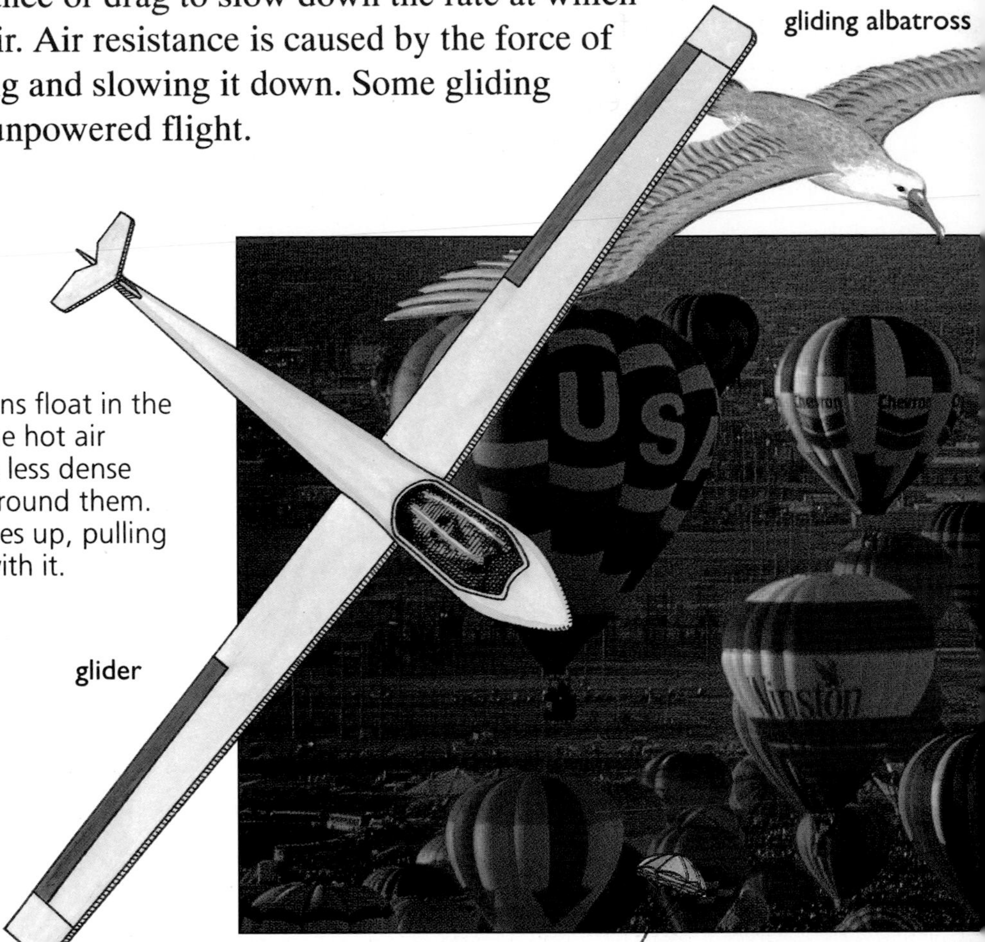

gliding albatross

Hot-air balloons float in the
air because the hot air
inside them is less dense
than the air around them.
The hot air rises up, pulling
the balloon with it.

glider

Feathered gliders

Some birds, such as vultures or storks,
soar and glide for hours on pockets of
rising hot air called thermals. Gliding on
thermals saves energy for birds on long
migration journeys. It also helps birds of
prey to stay up in the air
for long periods while
they search for food on
the ground below.
Seabirds, such as
albatrosses or gulls,
glide upwards on air
currents rising from
the waves or
cliffs.

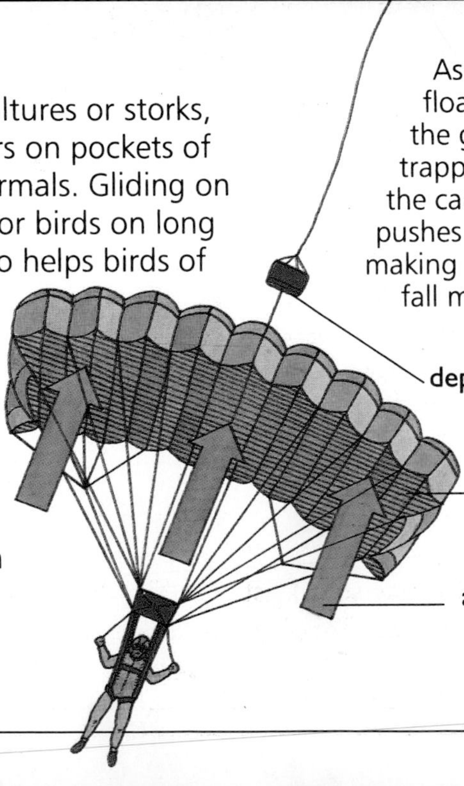

As a parachute
floats down to
the ground, air is
trapped under
the canopy. The air
pushes upwards,
making the 'chute
fall more slowly.

deployment bag

canopy

air resistance

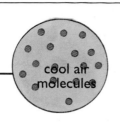

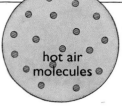

cool air molecules

hot air molecules

Hot air rises

When air is heated, its molecules gain energy and move further apart. This makes the hot air take up more space and become less dense, or 'lighter', than cool air. So the warm air rises above the cool air.

Design a glider

See if you can build a model glider of your own following these instructions. You will need card, scissors, tape, a knitting needle and straws.

1. Cut out the wings, the tail and five flaps from the card.

2. Stick on the flaps with tape to match the diagram.

3. Push a straw through the wings to make them bend on top, like real wings.

4. Use a knitting needle for the body of the glider and fix the tail to the needle with a bit of straw.

5. Bend the flaps up and down to change the glider's flight path.

Gliding animals

Gliding animals such as flying squirrels (above) or tree frogs use air resistance to help them fall slowly through the air. They have developed webs or flaps of skin which they spread out like living parachutes. The air pushes up against the skin flaps and slows down their falling speed. Flying fish glide over the waves for about 500m to escape predators. A gliding mammal called the flying lemur glides up to 135m between rainforest trees in southeast Asia. On the ground, its folded 'wings' get in the way and it cannot even stand up.

Flying frogs have enormous webbed feet to glide up to 12m when jumping from tree to tree.

ANIMAL FLIGHT

The first flying animals on Earth were probably insects, which flitted through the air hundreds of millions of years ago. During the days of the dinosaurs, flying reptiles called pterosaurs darkened the skies. Nowadays, only birds, bats and insects are capable of powered flight with controlled movements. Flying animals have many adaptations to help with flight, such as broad, flat wings, powerful wing muscles, lightweight bodies and a streamlined shape.

Vampires

The vampire bat lives in Central and South America. It bites mammals and birds to feed on their blood, but does not usually feed on humans. Although vampires can spread diseases, such as rabies, they do not usually kill the animals they feed on. Vampire bats have given rise to legends such as that of Count Dracula, made famous in the book by Bram Stoker.

A bird's wing is an aerofoil shape – curved on top and flat underneath. This creates a pressure difference during flight which pulls the bird upwards.

fruit bat

Bats are the only mammals able to power their own flight instead of just gliding. Their wings are made of skin stretched tight over the bones of their arms. Some bats have a flap of skin around the tail bone as well. They spread out this tail flap to help them steer through the air.

Flying reptiles

About 200 million years ago, when dinosaurs roamed the Earth, other reptiles took to the air. They were called pterosaurs, meaning 'winged reptiles', and ranged from the size of a sparrow to the size of a small aeroplane.

Their long, tapering wings were made of skin and their bones were lightweight and hollow. Some pterosaurs had long tails for steering, like a rudder on a ship.

blue tit

Bird wings

As well as flapping their wings, birds twist and turn them and change the angle of the feathers. As the wings beat down, the feathers overlap, so no air can pass through. This creates a large area to push against the air. As the bird pulls its wings up again, the feathers twist slightly apart so air can flow through. This means the bird uses less energy pushing against the air.

feathers closed on downstroke

feathers open on upstroke

Wings and lift

Animal wings beat down on the air, moving the animals forwards and sometimes upwards, but the shape of wings is also very important. The top of the wing is often curved, causing air to move faster over the top than beneath. This creates low pressure on top and high pressure below the wing. Air moves from high to low pressure areas, so the wing is 'sucked' upwards, giving the animal 'lift'.

Bees and wasps join each pair of wings together with rows of tiny hooks. This gives them two bigger wings to push against the air.

Insect wings

The wings of flying insects, such as butterflies, moths, wasps, beetles and flies, are made of thin, flat membranes, strengthened by small veins. The first flying insects on Earth had two pairs of wings which moved independently in flight; dragonflies fly like this today. Many modern insects (like flies) find it easier to fly with two wings. Beetles (like the Cockchafer beetle, right) have four wings, but the front ones are actually horny shields which protect the thin flying wings.

Musical flight

See if you can find pieces of music about flight and floating, such as 'The Flight of the Bumblebee' by the Russian composer Rimsky-Korsakov or the popular tune 'Fly me to the Moon'. Can you use everyday objects to create your own songs about flying to faraway places ?

FLYING MACHINES

People dreamed of flying for centuries, but flight has only been possible in the last hundred years. In that time, aircraft have developed from small wood and fabric planes to the gigantic jumbo jets and supersonic aircraft of today. Great leaps in speed and design were made during wartime as people tried to build better fighting planes. But modern planes still work on the same idea of aerofoil-shaped wings creating enough lift to support the weight of the aircraft and keep it up in the air.

air pressure drops above wing

lift

air pressure remains same below wing

Controlling an aircraft
A typical aircraft is controlled by movable flaps, called control surfaces, which allow the pilot to make the aircraft turn, climb and dive. On the wings are ailerons, on the back edge of the tail wings (the tailplane) are elevators, and on the upright part of the tail (the tail fin) is a rudder.

The ailerons on the wings are used together with the rudder to make the aircraft turn in the air. By moving the elevators, the pilot can make the aircraft climb or dive.

Jet engines
Most modern, high-speed aircraft are pushed along by jet engines. Fans at the front of the engine suck in air like a vacuum cleaner but at very great speed. Inside, the air is compressed in a series of turbines, sprayed with fuel and set on fire. The hot gases rush out of the back of the engine, pushing the aircraft forwards. It's rather like letting the air out of a balloon to make it zoom through the air.

Helicopters
Helicopters can twist and turn in the air rather like insects. They are much more manoeuvrable than an aeroplane, but they use up a lot of energy when they fly. Their aerofoil-shaped rotors produce lift as they spin around, so a helicopter does not have to speed fast through the air to create lift like an aeroplane. To move up or down, forwards or backwards, the angle of the rotor blades is adjusted.

The tail rotor stops helicopters spinning around by balancing the turning movement of their main rotors.

F-14 Tomcat

BAe 146

Concorde

Wing types

Concorde has a streamlined delta-shape wing to allow it to cruise at speeds of 2,300 kph, but it requires a long runway for take off. In contrast, the BAe 146 is designed for the short runways of city airports, its stubby wings giving maximum lift at take off. The F-14 Tomcat has the best of both worlds with its swing-wing technology. This allows it to swivel its main wings forward for extra lift on take off from aircraft carriers. In fast flight, the wings are swung backwards to form the aerodynamic delta wing shape.

Wind tunnel tests

In wind tunnels, smoky air is sucked over scale models (such as the one of Concorde below) to show the pattern of airflow over the surfaces of the aircraft. Designs can then be altered to reduce the amount of drag caused by tiny whirlwinds or eddies of air formed as the air flows over and around the body surfaces.

Flying into history

Since the first record-breaking aeroplane flight by the Wright brothers in 1903, many people have flown their way into the history books. Some have crossed oceans or mountains, others have broken speed or distance records.

Red Baron's triplane

1909 Louis Blériot flew across the English Channel in 36 minutes.
1919 First non-stop flight across the Atlantic by Alcock and Brown in a Vickers Vimy in 16 hours 27 minutes.
1927 Charles Lindbergh made the first solo flight across the Atlantic.
1930 Amy Johnson became the first woman to fly solo from England to Australia.
1932 Amelia Earhart was the first woman to fly the Atlantic alone.
1936 Amy Johnson completed a return flight from England to South Africa in 8 days.
1937 The first fully pressurised aircraft, the Lockheed XC-35, came into service.
1939 Igor Sikorsky designed and built the first helicopter.
1949 The De Havilland Comet, the first jet airliner, entered service. James Gallagher made the first non-stop flight around the world.
1969 Concorde was the first passenger plane to fly faster than the speed of sound.
1970 The Boeing 747 jumbo jet entered service.
1976 The world air-speed record of 3,529kph was set in California.
1986 First non-stop flight around the world without refuelling.
2000 British Airways is the world's busiest airline, carrying 31.2 million international travellers.

McDonnell Douglas MD-12

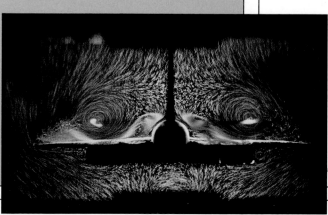

AIR AT WORK

We use air to improve our quality of life, both at home and at work. Many recipes mix air or gases with the ingredients, and fizzy drinks contain bubbles of carbon dioxide gas. Home appliances such as vacuum cleaners and tumble driers all make use of the properties of air. Air bags improve safety on cars and coaches (above right). In industry, air is used to keep things warm or cool, to extract harmful fumes or dust, and to burn things. Compressed air is a powerful source of safe energy for pneumatic tools.

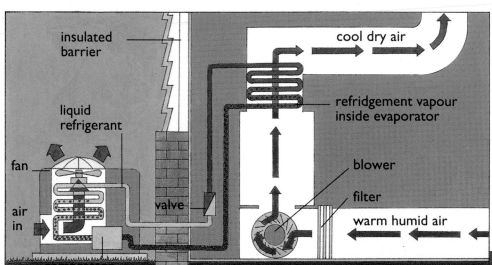

insulated barrier

liquid refrigerant

fan

air in

valve

compressor

cool dry air

refridgement vapour inside evaporator

blower

filter

warm humid air

Air conditioning
Inside an air conditioner a fan extracts air from the room. A liquid called a refrigerant turns into a gas (evaporates), taking heat from the air as it does so. The heat is released outside and the cool air returns to the room. The refrigerant gas is compressed to turn it back into a liquid so it can be used again.

Air in cooking
A lot of the food we cook is full of air. The bubbles in bread and cakes are carbon dioxide gas. This comes from yeast in bread-making or from baking powder or bicarbonate of soda in cakes. The bubbles expand on cooking to make the bread and cakes rise and give them a light, spongy texture. If bread is baked without yeast, it won't rise, producing unleavened bread. Mousses, meringues and soufflés are light and fluffy because of all the air whisked into them.

Expanded Polystyrene

Expanded polystyrene is a kind of plastic with lots of air bubbles in it. The air does not carry heat well, so polystyrene makes a good insulating material. It is also often used for packaging (left) because it is light yet rigid.

Airbrush art

An airbrush sprays air and ink to produce a flat, even colour. The air comes from a compressed air supply called a propellant, which may be an aerosol can or an electric air compressor plugged into the mains. As compressed air blows across the nozzle, it creates a vacuum. This sucks ink up a tube to fill the vacuum, creating a spray of air and ink.

An air supply valve controls the air flowing through the nozzle, allowing detailed work.

Making iron and steel

Blast furnaces (below) extract iron from a rocky material called iron ore. They are named after the blast of hot air that heats up the raw materials – iron ore, limestone and coke – inside the furnace. As the coke burns, it produces chemicals which take oxygen from the iron ore, leaving iron metal behind. The iron metal melts and sinks to the bottom of the furnace. Most iron is converted into steel.

Double glazing

One third of the heat in a building escapes through the walls, a quarter is lost through the roof and the rest gets out through the floors and windows. To prevent this loss of heat, buildings need to be well insulated. Double-glazed windows sandwich air between two layers of glass to hold in the heat. Insulating materials with lots of air pockets can be used to line the walls and roof. Cavity walls (two parallel walls joined by ties with an airspace in between) are sometimes filled with foam polystyrene.

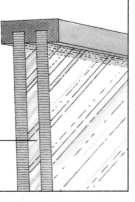

air trapped between the glass

Squashing air

When air is squashed or compressed into a small space, it can be used to provide a safe source of energy for power tools, called pneumatic tools. There is no danger of sparks to start fires and no chance of getting an electric shock. It works well for rotary tools such as dentists' drills where the compressed air is forced against a rotor with several blades. Compressed air is also used to inflate tyres and work air brakes.

The pressurised air under a hovercraft lifts it off the ground.

AIR POLLUTION

The Earth's atmosphere is polluted naturally by sandstorms and the dust and gases from volcanoes. But the most serious kind of air pollution comes from people. Factories, power stations and vehicle exhausts pump harmful gases into the air, contributing to global warming, causing acid rain and destroying the ozone layer. On a much smaller scale, air pollution causes all sorts of breathing problems. There are no simple solutions to air pollution, but people could reduce air pollution by saving energy and reducing harmful emissions from vehicle exhausts and power stations.

Noise pollution
Loud noises not only annoy people but can damage hearing. Noise is measured in decibels, with 0 decibels being the lowest sound audible to human ears. A level of 160 decibels, such as the noise of a jet aeroplane taking off at close range, will cause damage to hearing.

Air pollution is at its worst over big cities where millions of people live, work and travel about in cars, buses and lorries. Factory chimneys can be fitted with devices to cut down air pollution, but this is expensive. If better public transport and cycle lanes were available in towns and cities, people would be less likely to use their cars, reducing the overall amount of pollution.

Smoking
Smoking cigarettes adds to the general levels of air pollution as well as damaging our health. Cigarette smoke contains chemicals that can cause cancer, a gas which stops oxygen being taken into the blood and a substance called nicotine which raises blood pressure and makes the heart beat faster. No-smoking areas cut down on this pollution and save non-smokers breathing in other people's cigarette smoke.

Volcanic pollution

When a volcano erupts, dust is blasted high above the troposphere and may take weeks to be carried around the world. It is above the weather zone, so cannot be washed out of the air by rain. It will eventually fall to Earth after a few years.

Radioactive pollution

In 1986, part of a nuclear reactor at Chernobyl in the Ukraine exploded, releasing dangerous radioactive pollution into the atmosphere. This was carried around the world by winds and rain, polluting countries many thousands of kilometres away. The radioactivity was passed on from plants, which took it from the air, to animals eating plants. People were also affected (such as young children) and health and farming problems persist today.

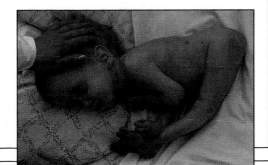

Detecting pollution

To find out more about the air pollution in your local area, try putting out squares of card covered in grease or vaseline. Put them in different places and leave them for a week or so. Which card collects the most dirt? How does the weather affect the amount of dirt in the air?

Plants called lichens are very sensitive to air pollution. If there are no lichens in your area, the air is very dirty. Leafy or bushy lichens indicate clean air, while the presence of flat, crusty lichens – like the orange circles on rooftops and walls – mean the air is really quite dirty.

particles in air stick to grease

FUTURE AIR

Retaining a viable atmosphere around the Earth for the future depends on reducing air pollution now. Otherwise problems such as ozone holes and acid rain can only get worse. Many of tomorrow's buildings and forms of transport will be designed with the environment in mind, for instance, using renewable sources of energy, such as solar power or wind power. Aircraft are likely to become even bigger and faster in the future, with supersonic flight becoming more widespread and aerodynamic design being an important consideration.

As well as being highly aerodynamic, the Maglev train uses magnetic fields to lift the train off the ground, reducing the energy needed for propulsion.

Clean CATs

One way of reducing the poisonous gases given off in exhaust fumes is to fit a catalytic converter or CAT. This changes toxic gases, such as carbon monoxide, hydrocarbons and nitrogen oxides, into less harmful gases, such as carbon dioxide, water and nitrogen. It reduces the harmful gases by up to 90 per cent.

A CAT is made of a coating of two metals, rhodium and platinum, on a honeycomb support. Lead sticks to rhodium and platinum, preventing the necessary chemical reactions from taking place. So cars with CATs must use lead-free petrol.

New sails

Modern sailing ships have sails designed to make the most efficient use of the wind. Some Japanese oil tankers (above) have computer-controlled sails as well as engines to help propel the ship and save on engine fuel.

The luxury five-masted yacht, the Club Med (right), has a more traditional appearance but uses the latest computer-aided technology and sail design to achieve maximum sailing efficiency. Land yachts driven by sails might be developed for travel across open country in the future.

The Lotus bike uses its flat frame as a sail to take advantage of cross winds.

Future aircraft

Jumbo jets are likely to get bigger in the future, perhaps even 'double jumbos', carrying 800 or more passengers on one flight. For long-distance travel, supersonic transport will become more common and space planes could reach speeds of Mach 20. New wing designs may be developed, building on the 'swing wing' designs of the fastest aircraft in the world today.

High-tech balloons may well become an important means of transport in the future. The Earthwinds Hilton (above) was designed for an around-the-world trip, expected to take 14 days. The crew will live in a 7-metre pressurised capsule made of glass-reinforced plastic.

New buildings

In the future, more buildings could be designed to use alternative energy, such as wind or solar power. The Tomigaya II project in central Tokyo (below) is designed to funnel and compress the prevailing winds towards a wind turbine, which turns to provide power. The tower on the right acts as a chimney to extract stale air from the building. Unfortunately the project was halted in the design stage and has not yet been completed.

AIR FACTS

Every time you breathe, about one-sixth of the air in your lungs is changed. If you are very fit, up to two-thirds can be changed.

Microscopic plants floating mainly in seawater produce more than 70 per cent of the Earth's oxygen.

The tuatara, an unusual reptile that lives in New Zealand, breathes only once every seven seconds when it

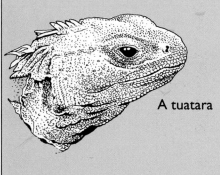

A tuatara

is moving and once an hour when it is resting.

The sort of cars we use on Earth need oxygen in the air to work. They won't work on the Moon, where there is no air. So astronauts had to use an electric car to explore the Moon.

When you sneeze air comes out of your lungs at over 160 kph – faster than the winds move in a hurricane.

The highest ever kite flew over 8,000m while the longest kite flight lasted for more than seven days.

A Peregrine falcon

Peregrine falcons can dive after their prey at speeds of almost 300kph.

In 1985, 99 American sky divers joined hands while falling down through the air. They made a star shape for 17 seconds.

The longest airship ever built was the *Hindenberg*. It was over three times longer than a jumbo jet and took

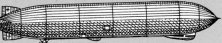

The *Hindenberg*

passengers across the Atlantic in 60 hours.

In the great London smog of 1952, over 4,000 people died from lung problems brought on by the smog and polluted air trapped in the city air.

Plant pollen (above) can travel up to 5,000km – far enough to cross the USA at its widest point.

Dandelion seeds can be carried by the wind for 10km. Orchid seeds also float like dust in the air. They are so light that 60 million of them weigh less than a postcard.

Mosquitoes flap their wings at over 500 beats a second. A very large bird, such as a swan, beats its wings only one and a half times a second.

A mosquito

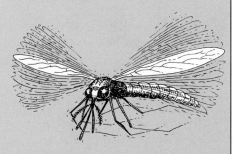

On a person's skin the air in the Earth's atmosphere exerts a total pressure of about 12,000kg.

The oxygen given off by the grass on a soccer pitch is used up by 70 soccer fans.

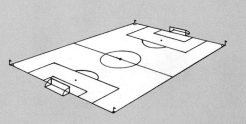

GLOSSARY

Aerofoil A wing that is curved on top and flat underneath.

Ailerons Flaps on the wings of an aeroplane that are moved up or down to make the aeroplane turn in the air.

Air pressure The weight of all the air in the atmosphere pressing down on the surface of the planet because of the pull of the Earth's gravity.

Air resistance or drag. The force of air pushing up against things, causing them to slow down or stop.

Alveolus (plural alveoli) An air cavity in the lungs.

Anticyclone The circulation of warm air around an area of high pressure which is usually associated with fine, settled weather.

Atmosphere The protective blanket of gases that surrounds the Earth or the layer of gases around any planet.

Catalytic converter (CAT) A device fixed to the exhaust system of a vehicle which removes most of the harmful gases produced by the engine before they can be released into the air.

Compressed air Air that has been squeezed into a small space.

Condensation The process by which a gas turns into a liquid as it cools down.

Density The mass of a substance per unit of volume. Mass is the amount of 'stuff' or matter a substance is made of.

Diaphragm A tough sheet of muscle separating the chest from the abdomen in mammals. It plays an important part in breathing movements.

Elevators Flaps on the tail of an aeroplane which can be moved to make it climb or dive through the air.

Frequency The number of sound vibrations per second, measured in hertz.

Gravity The force of attraction between any two objects. The size of the force depends on the size of the object. The Earth is enormous so has a huge gravitational pull.

Humidity The amount of water vapour in the air.

Insulator A material, such as air, that does not let heat pass through it easily.

Lift The force of air pressing up against things which keeps them up in the air.

Molecules The smallest particle of a substance that can exist by itself and still have the properties of that substance.

Photosynthesis The process by which plants use the Sun's energy to make their own food.

Respiration A chemical process which takes place inside the cells of living things. During respiration, food is 'burnt' in the presence of oxygen to release energy.

Stoma (plural stomata) A small hole in the surface of a plant leaf which controls the flow of gases and water vapour in and out of the leaf.

Thermal A current of air that rises because it is hot.

Vacuum A completely empty space with nothing inside it.

Water vapour The invisible gas that water changes into when it is heated.

INDEX

Photographic credits

Abbreviations: t – top, m – middle, b – bottom, l – left, r – right
Front cover t, 2t & b, 3b, 4ml, 9m, 11b, 14-15, 18-19, 20m & b, 23t all, 24-25, 26-27, 27b, 29bl: Frank Spooner Pictures; cover b, title page, 2m, 4mr, 5 all, 7b, 12tl, 113, 13t & b, 16t, 18t, 20t, 24bl, 25t & m: Roger Vlitos; 3m, 4br: Hulton Deutsch Picture Library; 4t, 13m, 14tl, 19b, 21b, 27t: Bruce Coleman Ltd; 6tr, 7t: NASA; 6b: Paul Nightingale; 8b, 9br, 11t, 16b, 17b: Spectrum Colour Library; 9bm: Charles de Vere; 22b: Julius Babasquone/ Solution Pictures; 23m & br: McDonnell Douglas; 23bl: British Aerospace; 24t: Ford UK; 25bl: USDA; 28t: Sikorsky Helicopters; 29t: Lotus Bikes; 29br: Richard Rogers Partnership.